EXPLORING OUR SOLAR SYSTEM

STAR SPOTTERS

TELESCOPES AND OBSERVATORIES

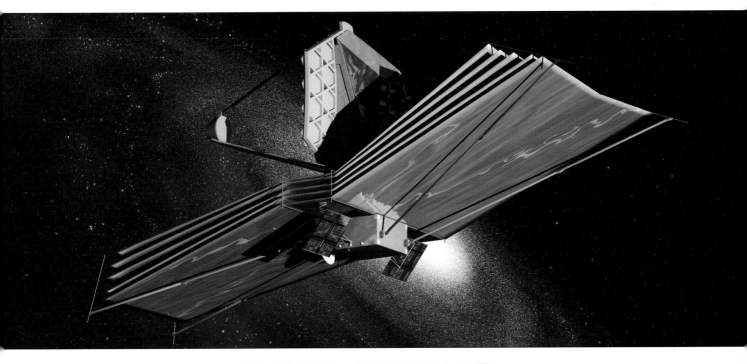

DAVID JEFFERIS

Crabtree

■STAR SPOTTERS

Modern astronomy started in 1608, when the first plans for a telescope were published by Hans Lippershey, a Dutch eyeglass-maker. His design was improved on by the Italian scientist Galileo Galilei, who became the first person to see such wonders of the night sky as the four biggest moons of Jupiter.

Today, astronomy is a cutting edge science that uses instruments that Lippershey or Galileo could not have imagined. The equipment astronomers use allows them to probe stars and events at the furthest frontiers of the universe.

Crabtree Publishing Company

PMB 16A,
350 Fifth Avenue, Suite 3308
New York, NY 10118

616 Welland Avenue,
St. Catharines, Ontario
L2M 5V6

Published by Crabtree
Publishing Company
© 2009

Written and produced by:
    David Jefferis/Buzz Books
Educational advisor: Julie Stapleton
Science advisor: Mat Irvine FBIS
Editor: Ellen Rodger
Copy editor: Adrianna Morganelli,
    Katherine Berti
Proofreader: Crystal Sikkens
Project editor: Robert Walker
Prepress technician: Margaret Salter
Production coordinator: Margaret Salter

■ ACKNOWLEDGEMENTS
We wish to thank all those people who have helped
to create this publication. Information and images
were supplied by:
Agencies and organizations:
    Association of Canadian Universities
    Australia National Telescope Facility/CSIRO
    California Institute of Technology
    CEA/Gornergrat Observatory
    ENO European Northern Observatory
    ESA European Space Agency
    ESO European Organisation for
        Astronomical Research in the
        Southern Hemisphere
    Gran Telescopio Canarias
    Hubble Space Telescope/STSci
    IAC Instituto de Astrofisica de Astrofisica
        de Canarias
    JPL Jet Propulsion Laboratory
    Large Binocular Telescope Observatory
    LSST Corp
    NAIC Arecibo Observatory, a facility
        of the NSF
    NASA National Aeronautics
        and Space Administration
    NSO National Solar Observatory
    NRAO National Radio Astronomy Observatory
    Palomar Observatory
    SAAO South African Astronomical Observatory

    SNO Sudbury Neutrino Observatory
    Sphinx Observatory
    Spitzer Science Center
    W. M. Keck Observatory
    Yerkes Observatory

Collections and individuals:
    Alpha Archive
    Mat Irvine
    iStockphoto/Diadem Images,
        fotoVoyager
    David Jefferis

Library and Archives Canada Cataloguing in Publication

Jefferis, David
    Star spotters : telescopes and observatories / David Jefferis.

(Exploring our solar system)
Includes index.
ISBN 978-0-7787-3725-4 (bound).--ISBN 978-0-7787-3742-1 (pbk.)

    1. Astronomical observatories--Juvenile literature. 2. Telescopes--Juvenile literature. 3. Radio astronomy--Juvenile literature. 4. X-ray astronomy--Juvenile literature. I. Title. II. Series: Jefferis, David . Exploring our solar system.

QB46.J43 2008   j522   C2008-907536-6

Library of Congress Cataloging-in-Publication Data

Jefferis, David.
    Star spotters : telescopes and observatories / David Jefferis.
        p. cm. -- (Exploring our solar system)
    Includes index.
    ISBN 978-0-7787-3742-1 (pbk. : alk. paper) -- ISBN 978-0-7787-3725-4 (reinforced lib. bdg. : alk. paper)
    1. Outer space--Exploration--Juvenile literature. 2. X-ray astronomy--Juvenile literature. 3. Telescopes--Juvenile literature. I. Title. II. Series.

    QB500.262.J44 2009
    522--dc22
                                                                                                    2008049242

CONTENTS

■WHEN DID PEOPLE FIRST OBSERVE THE SKIES?

No one knows who the first star spotters were, but we do know that observing the sky was important to all ancient peoples.

■ Stonehenge is a stone circle in England, built more than 4,000 years ago. The stones are lined up in the correct directions to show events such as the longest and shortest days of the year.

■ This astrolabe is a finely made brass instrument. It dates from the year 1569.

■ EARLY ASTRONOMERS

Ancient civilizations noted the movements of the stars and the Sun, because this helped them to predict the seasons, and know when exactly to plant their crops. Many ancient buildings were religious temples as much as places to study the heavens. The earliest star-gazing observatories were built in the Middle East, in Iraq and Iran, around 800-900 A.D.

WOW!
Early sky watchers did some very precise work. For example, the Arab scientist Al Battani determined the precise length of a year, to the exact second.

■ WHAT INSTRUMENTS DID THEY USE?

The early astronomers did not have telescopes. They studied the sky with their eyes. They made some sophisticated instruments to help them. By 1200 A.D., astronomers were using the astrolabe, which could locate and even predict the positions of the Sun, the Moon, some of the planets, and many of the brighter stars.

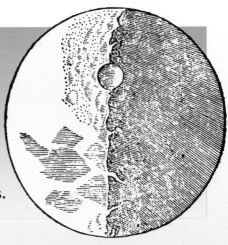

■ Galileo's most powerful telescope only enlarged 30 times. No matter, he saw craters on the Moon (right), and in 1610, he spotted Jupiter's four biggest moons.

■ WHO FIRST SKETCHED THE MOON?

The first telescope drawings of the Moon were made by the Italian scientist Galileo. In 1610, he published his sketches in a newsletter called the *Sidereus Nuncius* (Starry Messenger), which made him famous all over Europe.

■ In 1789 the world's biggest telescope (1) was the 40 ft (12 m) long instrument of English astronomer Sir William Herschel.

■ The Sphinx observatory (2) was built in 1937, high up on a Swiss mountain ridge called the Jungfraujoch. It is 11,417 ft (3,480 m) high. The Sphinx is still used regularly.

■ WHY ARE OBSERVATORIES SO OFTEN BUILT ON MOUNTAINTOPS?

Mountain observatories are above as much of the **atmosphere** as possible. Clouds, haze, dust, and air currents spoil a telescope's view of the night sky. Mountains are also among the best places to get really dark skies, away from the lights of big cities.

■WHY IS MUCH OF THE UNIVERSE INVISIBLE?

Stars pour out a huge range of energy, but we can sense only some of this. The small part that we can see is called visible light.

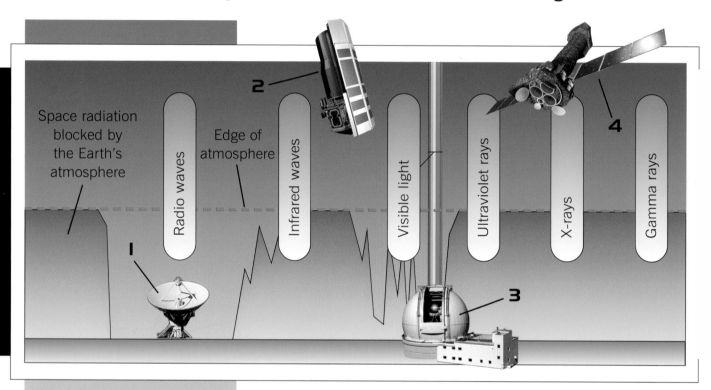

Space radiation blocked by the Earth's atmosphere

Edge of atmosphere

Radio waves

Infrared waves

Visible light

Ultraviolet rays

X-rays

Gamma rays

1

2

3

4

■ **Big antennas (1) detect radio waves. A special space telescope (2) detects infrared heat radiation. Ground observatories (3) use visible light. Space telescopes (4) can detect other radiation.**

■ WHAT MAKES UP THIS ENERGY RANGE?

The range of energy in nature is called the **electromagnetic spectrum** (EMS). This is a huge sweep of electrical and magnetic vibrations, called radiation. Low-energy radio waves are at one end of the EMS, visible light is in the middle. At the far end are high-energy waves such as gamma rays.

WOW!
Infrared and ultraviolet are "next door" to visible light. This allows some visible light equipment to be used to research these parts of the EMS.

■ WHAT ARE THE TWO MAIN BRANCHES OF ASTRONOMY TODAY?

Astronomers observe the universe in two basic ways. Optical instruments detect visible light. Non-optical astronomy deals with other parts of the EMS, such as radio waves or X-rays.

■ WHY IS IT USEFUL TO SEE MORE THAN VISIBLE LIGHT?

Quite simply, the more we can find out about a space object, the more we can learn about it, and then understand it better. Stars and **galaxies** often appear dramatically different when viewed with non-optical equipment. The three pictures below show the same group of stars!

This is the Andromeda galaxy, a vast spiral of more than 1,000 million stars

Dust trails show up in infrared

Infrared reveals the galaxy's **core** very clearly

■ These three pictures show the same Andromeda galaxy, viewed in visible light (top), and two levels of infrared energy. Images like these are often combined into one to show far more detail than you can get by viewing just one energy level.

■ WHAT ARE HIGH-ENERGY TELESCOPES?

These are instruments that can detect the most powerful radiation of all. Gamma rays are signs of massive star explosions, and galaxies ripping each other apart. **Cosmic rays** come from all sorts of places – some are from the Sun, others hurtle toward us from distant parts of the universe. In fact, cosmic rays are misnamed. They are actually particles that move across space.

■HOW FAST DOES LIGHT TRAVEL THROUGH SPACE?

It moves very quickly. Light and other forms of radiation speed through space at 186,000 miles per second (300,000 km/sec).

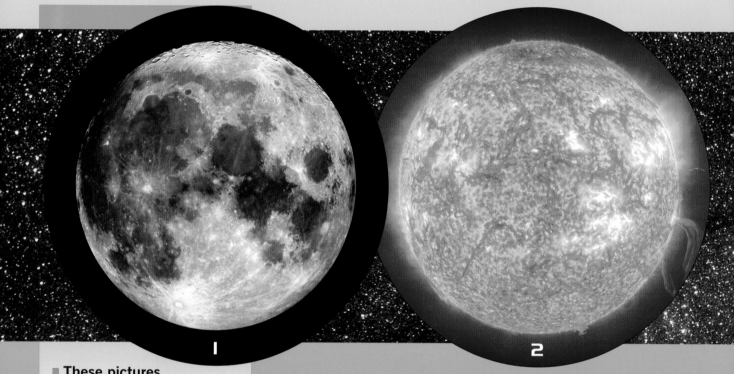

1

2

■ These pictures go from near Earth to the edge of the universe. Light from the Moon (1) is reflected from the Sun (2), our star at the center of the solar system.

■ HOW LONG DOES LIGHT TAKE TO REACH US?

Space is BIG, so light takes time to arrive, even from nearby space objects. The Moon is just 239,000 miles (385,000 km) from Earth. Even so, reflected sunlight from the Moon takes 1.3 seconds to reach us.

■ SO WHAT ABOUT STARLIGHT?

Our Sun is the nearest star, and is 93 million miles (150 million km) away. Its light takes 8.3 minutes to reach us. Beyond the solar system, distances are so great that they are measured in **light years**. One light year is a mind-boggling 5.9 trillion miles (ten trillion km)!

WOW!
From 1989-93 the ESA Hipparcos **satellite** made the first star position map from a spacecraft. Hipparcos mapped more than a million stars.

■ HOW DISTANT ARE OTHER STARS?

Apart from the Sun, the nearest stars are Alpha, Beta, and Proxima Centauri, a group that is just over four light years away. Even this is only next door in terms of space distances. The Milky Way galaxy, the "star city" in which the solar system moves, is 100,000 light years across. Beyond the Milky Way are billions of other galaxies.

■ The nearest star beyond the Sun is Proxima Centauri (3), depicted here in a fantasy illustration. The other two Centauri stars are to Proxima's right. The yellow blobs (4) are distant galaxies. They are more than 13 billion light years away.

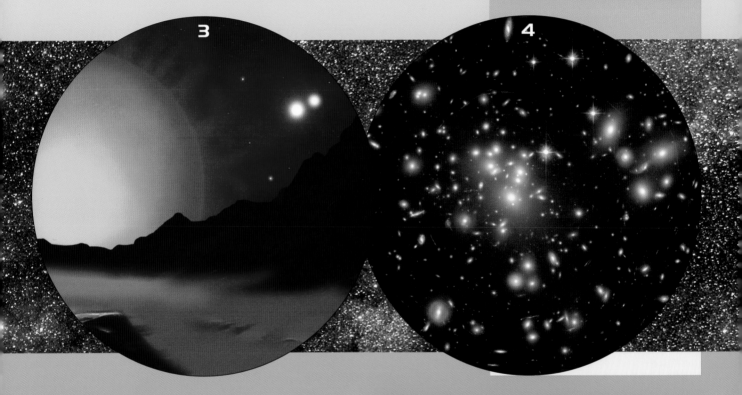

■ HOW FAR CAN WE SEE INTO THE DEPTHS OF THE UNIVERSE?

Galaxies have been viewed at about 13 billion light years away. Seeing them is like traveling back in time. The light is old and has taken 13 billion years to reach us.

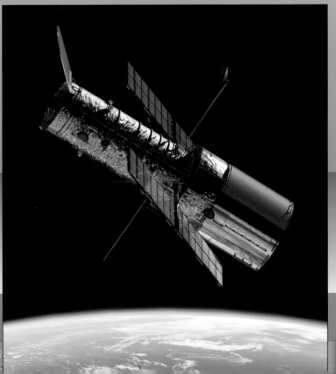

■ The Hubble Space Telescope (HST) has been one of the best star spotters ever built. Moving high above the Earth, the HST has taken thousands of deep-space pictures since 1990, including the distant galaxies shown above.

■ HOW DOES AN OPTICAL TELESCOPE WORK?

There are two basic telescope designs: refractor and reflector. For both types, the first essential task is to gather as much light as possible.

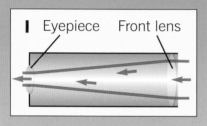

I Eyepiece   Front lens

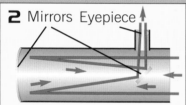

2 Mirrors Eyepiece

■ A refractor telescope (1) uses a front lens to gather light (red lines). A reflector telescope (2) uses a primary mirror for this. There are different sorts of telescope design, but they are all refractors or reflectors.

■ HOW DO DIFFERENT TELESCOPES WORK?

A **refractor** telescope has a big lens at the front to collect and concentrate light. A **reflector** telescope (below) uses a mirror to do this. Many small telescopes are refractor designs. Super-accurate mirrors are easier and cheaper to make than big lenses, so almost all big telescopes are reflectors.

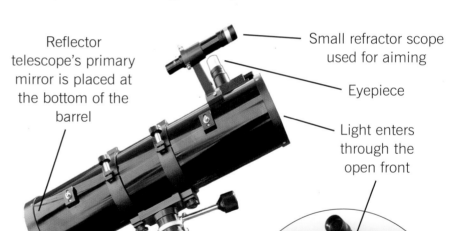

Reflector telescope's primary mirror is placed at the bottom of the barrel

Small refractor scope used for aiming

Eyepiece

Light enters through the open front

Strong tripod gives firm support

A secondary mirror reflects light from the main mirror sideways to the eyepiece

■ WHAT HAPPENS TO LIGHT WHEN IT HAS BEEN GATHERED?

The actual viewing of an image is made through the eyepiece. This straightens the light rays and acts as a magnifying glass. In all but the simplest telescopes, eyepieces come in various types, to suit the viewing conditions needed by different space objects.

■ 10

■ WHAT ABOUT THE BIGGEST TELESCOPES?

These are almost all reflectors. Big, heavy mirrors may bend under their own weight or with changes in temperature and distort images. However, results can be improved with the latest **active optic** technology. An active mirror is thin enough to bend when pushed from behind by mechanical levers. Computer control allows the shape of the mirror to be adjusted slightly, to give a near-perfect result.

■ Behind the sliding doors of the Palomar Observatory in California is the Hale 200-inch (5.08-m) reflector (top right). The Hale dates from 1948, when it was the world's largest telescope.

■ Here the main mirror is being made for the LSST, a telescope that will operate from Chile in 2015. The mirror is 27.5 ft (8.4 m) wide.

■ARE BIG TELESCOPES BETTER THAN SMALL ONES?

A big mirror collects more light than a small one, so it can detect fainter images. Quality is important too, which makes big telescopes very expensive.

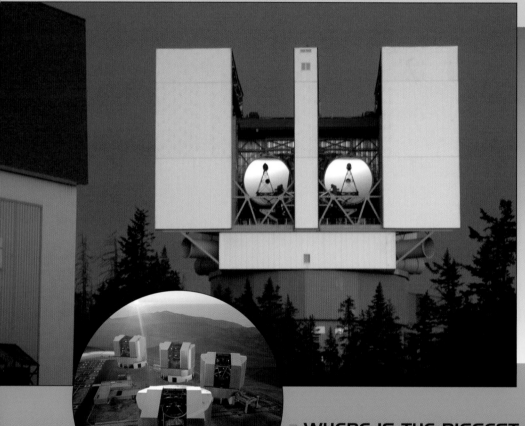

■ Sliding shutters protect the mirrors of the Large Binocular Telescope. Each mirror is 27.5 ft (8.4 m) across, but together they are as powerful as a single mirror nearly 39 ft (11.8 m) across.

■ In Chile, four telescopes (1) of the Very Large Telescope (VLT) work together as a team. The Southern African Large Telescope (2) has one big 36-ft (11-m) mirror.

1

2

▢ WHERE IS THE BIGGEST TELESCOPE?

The Large Binocular Telescope is at Mount Graham in Arizona, U.S.A., a place that has very clear skies. This optical telescope has not one, but two mirrors. Their images are combined as one, much like an ordinary pair of binoculars.

▢ DO OTHER COUNTRIES HAVE BIG TELESCOPES?

Yes — astronomy is a world-wide science, and telescopes are usually built where viewing is best. The biggest single mirror is 36 ft (11 m) across. It belongs to the Southern African Large Telescope (SALT), which was built in South Africa by a group of six countries.

Big mirrors have to be mounted firmly to avoid any vibration. Here the mounting cage of the world's number three telescope, the Gran Telescopio Canarias (GTC), is ready to receive the 34-ft (10.4-m) mirror.

HOW MUCH DOES A TELESCOPE COST?

The biggest telescopes are extremely costly. South Africa's SALT telescope cost around $26 million to construct, and has many specially-made parts. For example, the mirror needed a 45-tons steel mounting to hold it steady. It costs one million dollars a year to run the telescope and support its science team. That's a lot of money, but amateur astronomers often make new discoveries using much cheaper equipment!

The GTC operates from the Canary island of La Palma. The GTC was built by Spain, Mexico, and the U.S.

Keck I and II are on the Hawaiian island of Mauna Kea. They work as a pair, for better performance.

WHAT IS "FIRST LIGHT?"

This is the name astronomers give to the moment when the latest telescope is trained on the sky for the first time. The big dome shutters slide open, the telescope moves smoothly, aiming at its first target star — and then **first light** falls on the mirror and into the eyepiece!

WOW!
Keck I and II each use a mirror divided into 36 parts or segments. Active computer control ensures that all the segments stay in precise position.

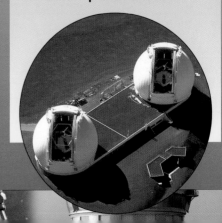

WHY IS RADIO ASTRONOMY SO IMPORTANT?

Radio waves form a big part of the electromagnetic spectrum. So observing the "radio sky" allows astronomers to learn more about deep space objects.

Karl Jansky steered his radio telescope by mounting it on vehicle wheels. The 100 ft (30 m) receiver could be turned slowly in a circle by hand.

WHO MADE THE FIRST RADIO TELESCOPE?

This was an American engineer called Karl Jansky. In 1931, he built a big **aerial** to research radio disturbances made during thunderstorms. He was successful in this, but he also recorded a strange background hiss, which seemed to be coming from the sky. Jansky found that the hissing sound was actually a faint "radio noise" coming from the millions of stars that make up our galaxy, the Milky Way.

WHY DO MOST RADIO TELESCOPES HAVE DISH-SHAPED RECEIVERS?

A radio telescope dish works much like the mirror of a reflector telescope. Radio waves are collected by the dish, then they are focused onto a smaller collector aerial. After this, the signals are displayed onscreen by computer equipment in the observatory. Most dishes are steerable, so that space objects can be tracked across the sky, to allow for the movement of Earth as it turns.

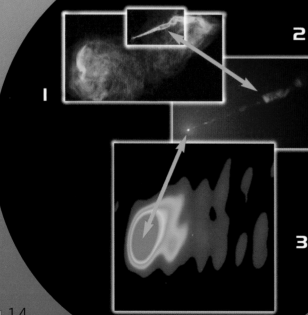

Here, radio noise from the distant galaxy M87 (1) reveals more detail than a visible light image (2), taken by the Hubble Space Telescope. Another radio telescope, called the VLBA, gives an even more detailed view of M87, with a close-up image (3) of its core zone.

WOW!
The first dish antenna was built in 1937 by Grote Reber. Using his 29.5 ft (9 m) dish, Reber carried out the first radio-sky survey.

WHY ARE RADIO TELESCOPES SO BIG?

This is because there is not as much information in a radio signal as in a light beam. To receive the same amount of detail that an optical telescope gets, a radio antenna has to be very large. Not all are dishes. Shapes and sizes vary from a long metal trough to an aerial much like a home TV antenna.

■ This is the 210-ft (64-m) Parkes radio telescope, in Australia. Three supports carry the receiver, above the big dish. Apart from radio astronomy, Parkes also tracks space probes as they explore the solar system.

■ This is the world's biggest radio telescope dish. It was made by building a giant receiver in a jungle hollow at Aricebo, on the Caribbean island of Puerto Rico. The dish is 1,000 ft (305 m) across, and was built in 1963.

■ HOW DO WE FIND OUT ABOUT THE SUN?

The Sun is one of the closest space objects to Earth, and can be studied from solar observatories on the ground or from high in space.

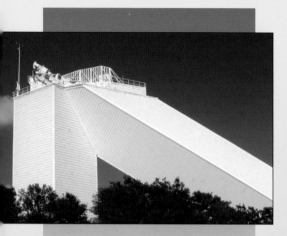

■ Scientists at the McMath-Pierce telescope can study an image of the Sun that is nearly 36 in (92 cm) across.

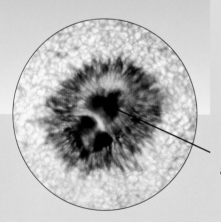

A sunspot's dark central area is called the umbra

■ WHAT IS INTERESTING ABOUT THE SUN?

It is the nearest star, and is what makes life on Earth possible. Studying how the Sun works gives more accurate weather forecasts. This helps farmers plant and harvest crops. Energy from the Sun may also affect delicate electronic systems, so Sun storm warnings help protect such equipment.

■ WHERE IS THE BIGGEST SOLAR TELESCOPE?

The telescope is called the McMath-Pierce Solar Telescope, at Kitt Peak, U.S.A. On top of a 100-ft (30-m) tower is a rotating mirror called a **heliostat**. This follows the Sun during the day, and reflects its image down a long sloping tube. At the bottom is a big viewing table. Scientists use the telescope mainly to study sunspots. These are cool areas that come and go on the Sun's surface.

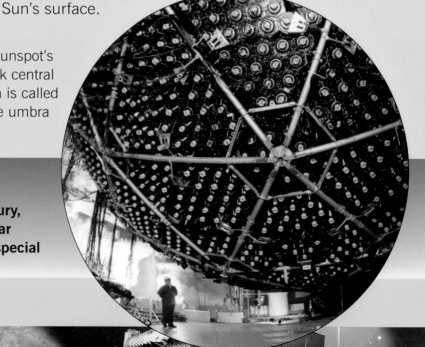

■ This massive sphere is part of a neutrino detector, built 6,800 ft (2,072.6 m) underground at Sudbury, Ontario, Canada. Neutrinos are solar particles that can be trapped in a special liquid that fills the high-tech ball.

■ SOHO is a 1,344-lb (610-kg) spacecraft that cruises in space about 930,000 miles (1.5 million km) from Earth. It sends information that warns of energy storms on the Sun, called solar flares. Other studies allow us to find out what's inside the Sun, as the diagram (left) shows.

WOW!
The first space telescope to look at the Sun was the Orbiting Solar Observatory (OSO). In total, eight OSOs were launched, from 1962 to 1975.

■ WHAT ABOUT VIEWING THE SUN FROM SPACE?

Knowledge of the Sun has advanced in leaps and bounds since the first solar observatories went into space in the 1960s. The most successful of them all has probably been the Solar Heliospheric Observatory (SOHO), which has been looking at the Sun since 1995. In that time, it has made many discoveries, with a mission that has included many studies of the Sun's outer and inner layers. SOHO also measures the **solar wind**, a stream of high-energy particles that pour out of the Sun, across the entire solar system.

■WHAT CAN THE HUBBLE SPACE TELESCOPE SEE?

Its observations have ranged from other planets in our solar system to far-off galaxies in deep space.

The Eagle nebula is 6,500 light years away from the Earth

■ WHAT IS THE HUBBLE'S MOST FAMOUS PICTURE?

The Hubble Space Telescope (HST) has taken thousands of pictures, but probably the best known is called the "Pillars of Creation" (left). The pillars are really vast clouds of gas and dust in the distant Eagle **nebula**. The black parts are areas that were not scanned by the camera.

■ HOW IS THE HST KEPT IN WORKING ORDER?

The HST is maintained by astronauts flying aboard the U.S. Space Shuttle. Special servicing missions are flown to the HST. Then astronauts go out on spacewalks, with replacement parts to keep the HST working.

■ Soon after its launch in 1990, scientists realized that the HST was not focusing sharply (1). The cause was the main mirror, which had been made to a slightly wrong shape. In 1993, astronauts installed a system to correct this. Since then the HST's images have been sharp and crisp (2).

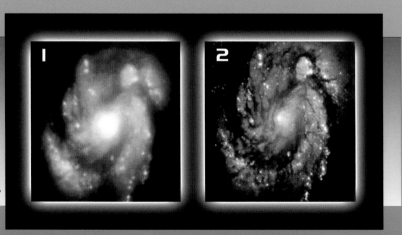

■ Astronauts worked on the HST during the first servicing mission of 1993. They fitted upgraded equipment and new solar panels.

■ The HST circles Earth at a height of 366 miles (589 km), where it is clear of any blurring effects caused by Earth's atmosphere.

HOW BIG IS THE HST?

The HST is about the same size as a school bus. On Earth, it would weigh more than 11 tons (10 tonnes). The telescope is a reflector design, with a main mirror 94 inches (2.4 m) across. Power to work the HST's many systems comes from two long solar panels, one mounted on each side. The panels are made of material that changes the energy contained in sunlight directly to electricity.

WOW!
There are traces of atmosphere even at HST's height, which affect its course slightly. Over a six-week period, HST's position may vary by up to 2,500 miles (4,000 km).

WILL THE HST BE REPLACED ONE DAY?

There are no plans for an exact replacement, but the new James Webb Space Telescope (JWST) will be able to carry out even more detailed observations.

WHERE DO WE LOOK FOR INFRARED TARGETS?

Much of the universe is filled with warm objects that are not hot enough to glow visibly, but they can be detected by their infrared radiation.

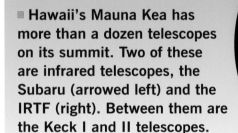

■ **Hawaii's Mauna Kea has more than a dozen telescopes on its summit. Two of these are infrared telescopes, the Subaru (arrowed left) and the IRTF (right). Between them are the Keck I and II telescopes.**

■ WHERE ARE THE BEST PLACES FOR INFRARED OBSERVATORIES?

Most infrared waves are absorbed by the atmosphere, so the best observatory spots are on mountains or in space. The summit of the Mauna Kea volcano in Hawaii has several telescopes. It is 13,800 ft (4,200 m) up, so about 90 percent of the atmosphere lies below the viewing zone. Despite the height, equipment has to be specially cooled, to avoid faint infrared signals being swamped by swirling air currents.

The Spitzer space telescope has searched for infrared objects since 2003

■ HOW BIG IS THE SPITZER SPACE TELESCOPE?

The Spitzer infrared space telescope weighed 2,090 lb (950 kg) when launched by a Delta II rocket. Spitzer has three instruments on board, all designed to record infrared radiation. The main telescope is 2.8 ft (85 cm) across, about the width of your outstretched arms. Unlike the Hubble Space Telescope, Spitzer does not circle the Earth. Instead, it trails behind us, moving around the Sun in a curving path called a heliocentric **orbit**.

WOW!
The Spitzer is one of the "Great Space Observatories" launched by the U.S. Space Agency, NASA. Others still in space are the HST and Chandra X-ray telescope.

1

2

3

■ WHAT HAS THE SPITZER FOUND?

Among Spitzer's first discoveries were planets circling other stars. These were a new kind of planet called a "hot Jupiter" — named because they are much warmer than the biggest planet in our solar system. They are not hot enough to glow visibly, like a star.

■ This picture combines information from the Hubble and Spitzer space telescopes. Infrared energy cuts through much of the gas and dust, so Spitzer can see things that the HST cannot view. In this specially-colored image, the "eyes" (1, 2) are the core zones of two colliding galaxies, 140 million light years away. The pink areas (3) are made of gases, dust, and millions of stars.

■ ARE THERE OTHER INFRARED TELESCOPES?

Spitzer was not the first infrared space observatory. In 1983, the IRAS satellite made the first infrared sky survey. In 2006, Japan launched its Akari probe, to carry on infrared studies.

■ Information from Spitzer showed that this four-star system has a huge ring of dust, circling two of the stars. The system, called HD98800, lies 150 light years away from Earth.

WHAT IS X-RAY ASTRONOMY?

X-rays are high-energy radiation that is beyond visible light.
There are several space telescopes equipped with X-ray detectors.

■ The XMM Newton space telescope was sent into space in 1999. XMM is 33 ft (10 m) long, weighs 8,818 pounds (3,999 kg), and carries three X-ray telescopes.

■ WHEN WERE SPACE X-RAYS DISCOVERED?

They were first spotted by high-flying research rockets, in the 1960s. X-rays in space came as a real surprise to scientists. The Earth's atmosphere is good at shielding us from X-rays (they can damage living cells), so they are completely invisible to ground-based telescopes.

WOW!
In 2007, XMM Newton saw X-rays blasted off a star called V598 Puppis, as it exploded. The visible-light flare brightened V598 more than 600 times.

■ WHAT DOES XMM NEWTON STUDY?

The Europe-U.S. XMM Newton was designed to observe high-energy X-rays from strange space objects, such as **pulsars** and active galaxies. A pulsar is a tiny star that spins at high speed. It pumps out a beam of radiation, much like a space lighthouse. An active galaxy has a central region pouring out massive amounts of energy into surrounding space.

Chandra was launched by space shuttle in 1999

The gas cloud is now ten light years across

Some gases are expanding at 90,000 miles per second (150,000 km/sec)

■ WHAT HAS CHANDRA SEEN?

Chandra is a U.S. X-ray telescope that has made many discoveries, including the sky's "brightest" radio object, Cassiopeia A (above). Cas A is a shell of gas and dust, marking the remains of a star that blew up in a huge explosion, 11,000 years ago. Cas A is a brilliant X-ray object, but can barely be seen in visible light.

■ There are closer targets for Chandra's X-ray eye to view. Here the planet Jupiter shows the auroras at its North and South poles. These electrical displays are bigger than all of Earth (arrowed).

■WHAT ARE ASTRONOMY'S NEW FRONTIERS?

New and more powerful telescopes will help astronomers see further into space. They might even find Earth-like planets circling other stars.

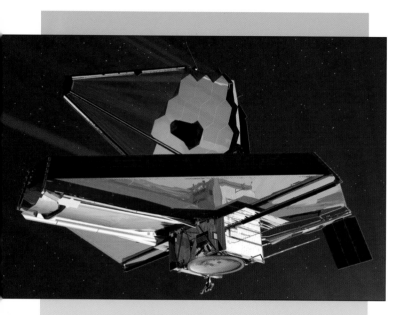

■ The JWST looks more like a spacecraft from a science fiction movie than a telescope. But its big mirror should allow scientists to see further into the universe than ever before, and far beyond the reach of even the biggest ground-based telescopes.

■ WHAT COMES AFTER THE HUBBLE SPACE TELESCOPE?

As planned, much of the HST's job will be taken over by the James Webb Space Telescope (JWST), which will have a main mirror 21 ft (6.4 m) across. Unlike the HST, the JWST will be an infrared telescope, which is better than visible light for observing many distant space objects. Infrared telescopes have to be kept very cold, so the JWST will have a fan-like shade. This will unfurl to shield the craft from the Sun's rays, and even from reflected moonlight.

WOW!
The JWST will have 62,000 micro-shutters, tiny devices that act like eyelashes. The micro-shutters will aid JWST's vision, just as we squint in bright light.

Technician works on a JWST test mirror assembly

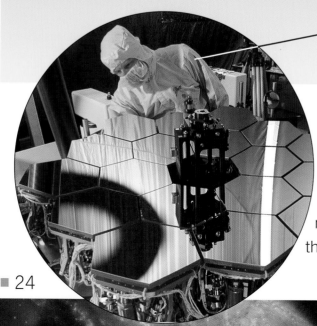

■ HOW BIG IS THE JWST DESIGN?

When launched from Earth, the JWST will weigh about half the Hubble's 11.3 tons (10.3 tonnes), but will have a mirror with more than six times more area. The mirror will be made of 18 segments that will unfold when the telescope is in space.

■ The Darwin project has plans for three infrared space telescopes, working together. The idea is to look for an Earth-like planet, perhaps like the artist's impression above.

■ WHAT IS THE DARWIN PROJECT?

This is a European plan for a planet-hunting space telescope. If built, Darwin's job will be to look for planets like Earth that may be circling other stars. If an "Earth 2" is found, scientists hope to find life there. It sounds like science fiction, but until 1992, no one knew of any planets beyond our solar system. Since that time hundreds have been found. We need super-scopes like Darwin to look for small planets like Earth.

■ The planners of the European Extra Large telescope (E-ELT) plan to build a ground-based telescope that can see better than the Hubble Space Telescope.
  If built, the E-ELT will have a huge segmented mirror, no less than 140 ft (42 m) across. Adaptive optics are an essential part of the telescope's design, used to reduce atmospheric blurring.

■HOW CAN I GO STAR SPOTTING?

You can start off easily, in the back garden or by joining a local astronomy club. For detailed study you need binoculars or a small telescope.

■ WHAT BINOCULARS ARE BEST FOR NIGHT SKY VIEWING?

All equipment comes with pros and cons, but if you need to buy a pair of binoculars, then the best type for night viewing is the traditional "big" design (below left). Look for binoculars marked 7x50, 8x50, or 10x50. The first number tells you how much they magnify — 7x is seven times bigger, and so on. In fact, you don't want a huge magnification, otherwise you will have trouble keeping the image steady. The second number is the width of the front lenses, in millimeters. Here, bigger is better as it means more light-gathering power, which is what all sky-watchers need!

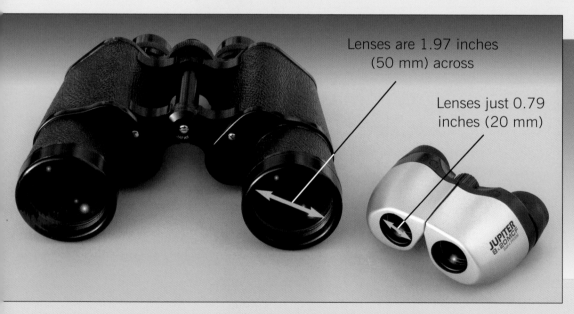

Lenses are 1.97 inches (50 mm) across

Lenses just 0.79 inches (20 mm)

■ The hefty black binoculars weigh 2.2 lb (one kg) but the big front lenses gather lots of light. The result is really good star spotting.

■ WHAT ABOUT POCKET-SIZE BINOCULARS?

What you lose on light-gathering power with these is gained by having them available more of the time. The 8x20 silver pair (above right) weighs just 5.6 oz (160 gr), and is pocket size and handy to carry around. It is not expensive, and is of very good quality. It is made by Pentax, one of Japan's top lens makers.

DANGER NEVER look at, or photograph, the Sun directly. The Sun is extremely bright, so looking closely will damage your eyes and wreck a camera.

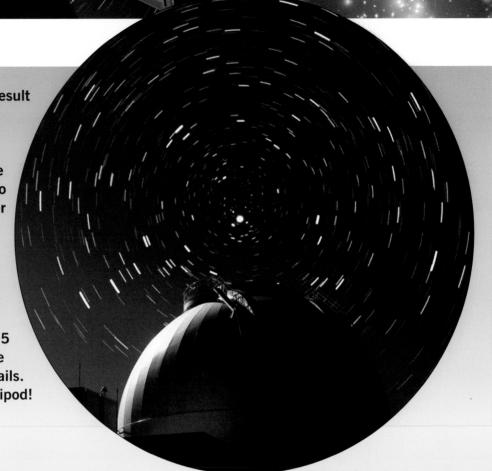

■ This is the sort of great result you can get with the right camera and a little care. Here the camera was pointed toward Polaris, the Pole Star, which appears to stay in the same place over the North Pole as the Earth turns beneath it.

The "star trails" show the Earth's rotation during the course of the camera's time exposure. Here the shutter was left open for 15 minutes. A longer exposure time would show longer trails. Remember to use a firm tripod!

■ WHAT EQUIPMENT DO I NEED TO PHOTOGRAPH THE STARS?

At its simplest, night sky photography needs no more than a camera and a tripod, or three-legged stand. The camera should have one basic item: a time exposure, or "bulb" setting. With this you can leave the shutter open to collect more light. The best plan is to start with a one-second exposure, then go up in steps to about a minute or so. Jot down your settings as you go. Many cameras do this automatically when a picture is taken. It is called the Exif information.

■ WHY IS A TRIPOD NEEDED?

A tripod keeps the camera steady. Without one, any exposure of more than about 1/30 of a second will be blurred – stars will show only as jiggly streaks. You do not need a big tripod like the one on page 10. A pocket-size item will do just fine.

■ Night photography sometimes gives you an interesting surprise. Here the camera was aiming at the Big Dipper star group, but it also captured the light of a satellite moving overhead. The flashing was caused by reflected sunlight, as the satellite turned in space.

■ FACTS AND FIGURES

■ HOW MANY SPACE TELESCOPES ARE THERE?

By 2008 no less than 98 space observatories of all types had been launched into space. Most are built to work for only a few years before systems fail or their power runs out.

■ WHAT IS THE BIGGEST REFRACTOR TELESCOPE?

This is the 40-inch (102-cm) telescope at the Yerkes Observatory, in Wisconsin. It was built in 1897, but even today is a regularly-used piece of equipment. Few big refractors are built today, although the 2002 Swedish Solar Telescope in the Canary Islands has a 39.4-inch (100-cm) collecting lens.

■ The Yerkes refractor is more than 100 years old, but it is still used. The telescope is 60 ft (18.3 m) long and weighs 44,092 pounds (20,000 kgs).

■ In 2017, the Thirty Metre Telescope (TMT) may see first light. It will be the biggest optical telescope, but the E-ELT may be bigger one day. Plans call for a TMT mirror made of 492 segments. The mirror will allow sky viewing up to 100 times better than anything used today.

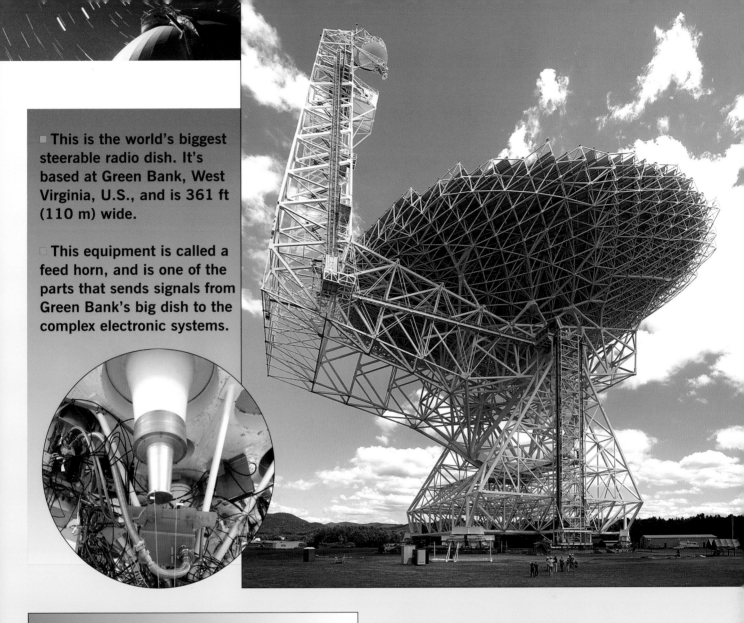

■ This is the world's biggest steerable radio dish. It's based at Green Bank, West Virginia, U.S., and is 361 ft (110 m) wide.

□ This equipment is called a feed horn, and is one of the parts that sends signals from Green Bank's big dish to the complex electronic systems.

WHERE ARE THE BIGGEST RADIO TELESCOPE DISHES?

The biggest of all is the 1,000-ft (305-m) dish at Arecibo, Puerto Rico. However, the dish does not move. A receiver assembly moves overhead on steel cables.

After Green Bank (see picture above), the biggest steerable radio telescope is the 328-ft (100-m) dish at Effelsberg, Germany, followed by the 250-ft (76-m) Lovell Telescope at Jodrell Bank, UK.

Even the biggest dish antenna is small, compared to other types of radio telescopes. Russia's Ratan-600 has 896 radio reflectors, placed in a circle, 1,890 ft (576 m) across. The angle of the reflectors can be adjusted, so that they beam radio signals to a receiver antenna in the middle.

WHAT IS AN ARRAY?

A radio telescope **array** is made by linking up lots of telescopes, to form a huge receiver as big as all of them put together. The Very Large Array (VLA) in New Mexico, U.S., links 27 dishes (below) in a huge Y-shape. The VLA is also part of a bigger network of radio telescopes, including the huge Green Bank dish shown above.

■ GLOSSARY

Here are explanations for many of the terms used in this book.

Active optics Computer-controlled systems that adjust a telescope mirror to improve viewing. Adaptive optics do a similar job, but using software rather than moving anything.

Aerial A device that receieves radio signals

Antenna Any electronic device that allows signals to be sent or received.

Array A group of radio telescopes that are linked together electronically, as a single unit. The advantage is that their receiving power becomes as powerful as the whole array.

Astrolabe Early astronomical instrument, used to predict the movement of various space objects.

Atmosphere The gases that make up the layers of air around the Earth, mostly nitrogen and oxygen.

■ Two early leaders of astronomy, Hans Lippershey (top) and Galileo Galilei.

■ Adaptive optics have enabled ground-based telescopes to compete with those in space. Here, a blurry image is uncorrected (1), then adjusted (2, 3) to reveal two stars.

Aurora A glow in the sky of a planet such as the Earth or Jupiter. Caused by particles from the Sun.

Core The center of a space object, such as a planet, a star, or a galaxy.

Cosmic ray High-energy particle, given off by the Sun and other stars.

Electromagnetic spectrum (EMS) All wave energy, including radio waves, infrared, visible light, ultraviolet, X-rays, and gamma rays. Known in general as radiation.

First light The name for the first time a telescope is used, when light from a space object is received.

Galaxy A huge group of stars. The solar system belongs to the Milky Way galaxy, which is thought to contain 200 to 400 million stars.

Part of the Sun to the same scale as the planets

1 2 3 4   5   6   7   8

Heliostat A moving mirror that can be angled to reflect sunlight in a particular direction.

Light year The distance that light covers in a year, traveling at a speed of 186,000 miles per second (300,000 km/sec).

Nebula A cloud of gas and dust in outer space.

Orbit The curving path of one space object around a bigger one. The Spitzer space telescope follows a heliocentric orbit, one that circles the Sun, like Earth and other planets.

Pulsar A spinning star that sends out a flashing beam of radiation.

Reflector A telescope that uses mirrors to collect light.

Refractor A telescope that uses lenses to collect light.

Satellite A space object that orbits another one. It may be a natural satellite, such as the Moon, or an artificial one, such as the HST.

Solar flare A violent energy explosion on the Sun.

Solar panel A flat panel made with silicon, a material that changes the energy in sunlight to electricity.

Solar system The name for the Sun, the eight major planets, several dwarf planets, and countless smaller space objects that circle it.

Solar wind The stream of particles blowing from the Sun across space throughout the solar system.

■ Here are the Sun and major planets:
1 Mercury
2 Venus
3 Earth
4 Mars
5 Jupiter
6 Saturn
7 Uranus
8 Neptune

■ GOING FURTHER

Using the internet is a great way to expand your knowledge of telescopes and astronomy. Your first visit should be to the site of the U.S. Space Agency, NASA. Its site includes the story of spaceflight and the universe in general. Here are two useful website addresses to start with:

www.nasa.gov   A huge space site.
www.space.com   Good space-news site.

Magazines, such as Astronomy, Astronomy Now, and Astronomy Today, also have websites.

■INDEX

Printed in the U.S.A.—CG